TRAUMA

National Touring Exhibitions

Published on the occasion of *Trauma*, a National Touring Exhibition organized by the Hayward Gallery, London for the Arts Council of England in collaboration with Dundee Contemporary Arts

Exhibition tour:
Dundee Contemporary Arts: 7 July – 2 September 2001
Firstsite, Colchester: 15 September – 17 November
Museum of Modern Art, Oxford: 25 January – 7 April 2002

Exhibition curated by Fiona Bradley, Katrina Brown and Andrew Nairne

Exhibition organized by Fiona Bradley and Sophie Allen

Catalogue designed by Esterson Lackersteen

Printed in England by The Beacon Press

Front cover: Kendell Geers, *Cry Wolf*, 1999 (cat. 8)

Frontispiece: Johan Grimonprez, still from *dial H-I-S-T-O-R-Y*, 1997 (cat. 13), 'Three hijacked jets being destroyed on desert airstrip at Amman, on September 12, 1970' Photography: Rony Vissers

Published by Hayward Gallery Publishing, London SE1 8XX, UK
© Hayward Gallery 2001
Artworks © the artists 2001 (unless stated otherwise)

The publisher has made every effort to contact all copyright holders. If proper acknowledgement has not been made, we ask copyright holders to contact the publisher.

ISBN 1 85332 219 9

Hayward Gallery Publishing titles are distributed outside North and South America and Canada by Cornerhouse Publications, 70 Oxford Street, Manchester M1 5NH (telephone 0161 200 1503; fax 0161 200 1504).

Exhibitions made in collaboration with partner organizations across the country are an important element of the Hayward Gallery's National Touring Exhibitions programme, and result in some of our most dynamic and stimulating projects. *Trauma* began as a conversation in Dundee Contemporary Arts about contemporary art's ability to make a space for the contemplation of serious social and personal issues and our joint desire to make an exhibition that took account of this.

Trauma explores some of the ways in which contemporary artists address the subject of trauma. The artists whose work is included in the exhibition are concerned both with the immediate experience of traumatic events and situations and with their profound personal, psychological, social, cultural and political repercussions and reverberations. They deal with the subject for a variety of reasons, and in a range of different ways. Some engage with specific situations as active participants, witnesses or commentators. Others make work that is more allusive, generating a situation for the potential of trauma within the work itself.

We are delighted to have had the opportunity to work closely with Dundee Contemporary Arts, and thank Andrew Nairne and Katrina Brown with whom our discussions around the theme began, and who have, together with Fiona Bradley of the Hayward Gallery, curated the exhibition and written this catalogue. The catalogue has been edited and produced by the Hayward Gallery, and I extend particular thanks to Linda Schofield, the Hayward Gallery's Art Publisher, and Caroline Wetherilt, our Publishing Coordinator, for their attention to it. My thanks also go to Simon Esterson for his design.

We are pleased that *Trauma* will be seen at the Museum of Modern Art in Oxford, where Andrew Nairne is now Director, and at Firstsite in Colchester, thanks to the enthusiasm of Kath Wood.

The exhibition has benefited from conversations with many of the artists involved and from their interest in and commitment to its subject. Our biggest debt of gratitude is to them, and to the lenders of work from public and private collections. A touring exhibition presents a particular challenge, and we are aware of the difficulties involved in parting with major works for a significant period of time. We thank everyone who has participated so willingly in the exhibition and in this publication, and trust that it proves a valuable assessment of this fundamental element of contemporary life.

Susan Ferleger Brades
Director, Hayward Gallery

Fiona Bradley
Katrina Brown
Andrew Nairne

'A trauma is something one repeats and repeats, after all…'
(Zadie Smith, *White Teeth*, Hamish Hamilton, London,
2000, p.140)

The word trauma rips through the English language much
as the situation it describes rips through the lives of those it
affects. Trauma indicates a caesura, necessitates a pause –
it arises from a moment of rupture, of radical disjunction.
It suggests an impact brought about by external forces,
something beyond the control of the individual and yet
having enormous, possibly immeasurable consequences.
This disparity between sudden arrival and long-ranging
affect may provide a clue to the fascination with trauma in
contemporary society. It offends our belief in the link between
empirical knowledge and control, our aspiration to order, our
assumptions of the logical, intelligible connection between
cause and effect. Trauma fractures the fragile webs that
provide the framework for our interface with the social,
political, cultural and emotional realms in which we function.

Derived from Greek, the word's original meaning is
'wound', and it retains that meaning in some contemporary
uses (in hospitals, for example, where trauma refers primarily
to physical damage). More frequently, however, it is used to
denote a psychological state resulting from a particular
event, with the event itself subsequently indicated by the
use of the same word. An individual is said to be in a state
of trauma because he or she has suffered a trauma, has
witnessed or undergone a traumatic event. The word
registers an emotional shock resulting from a significant
physical or psychological dislocation, often unexpected
and always unpleasant, over which the subject has no
control. It describes an event and its impact, or rather an
event in terms of its impact.

Although it is part of the vocabulary of contemporary
emotion, the term derives much of its weight from its status
within psychoanalytic discourse as the primary cause of
neuroses within the Freudian account of the psychosexual
development of the individual. In the simplest understanding
of psychoanalysis, the subject attempts to recover memory
and understanding of the traumatic event or situation that
dominates his or her present mental state. Crucially, for
Freud, an event is registered as traumatic only when it is
revisited at a later date, when it is 're-coded' through some
subsequent mental or physical action. This is perhaps most

familiar in the analysis of dreams, where subconscious
recurrences are seen as inventive and interminable
reworkings of the trauma, the main elements of which
are concealed somewhere in the language the individual
uses to describe the dream.

The tenets of psychoanalysis have entered contemporary
discourse at the level of language, and as the basis for our
willingness to accept that an individual may be
psychologically as well as physically affected by external
events. We acknowledge the existence of post-traumatic
stress syndrome, and the likelihood that people may be
'traumatized' by experiences they have had or witnessed.
We seek the signs in soldiers, fire officers, police and social
workers as well as in the victims of the situations to which
these people are routinely exposed. We understand the
effects of trauma to be both immediate and long-lasting,
and also relative, so that individuals may react differently
to the shared experience of the same event.

Trauma may be discussed both in individual and
collective terms. Divorce, disease, torture and death affect
individuals, as do famine, flood and war. Yet when
individual suffering is magnified to become a national or
international disaster, trauma begins to take hold of the
collective imagination. This process is, of course, inspired
and manipulated by the media. National events are
characterized as moments of multiple trauma as they
are photographed, filmed and written about, and as the
original situation is repeated simultaneously on millions
of televisions throughout the world. It is often only through
the media that we become aware of such situations, both
close to home and further afield, and our ease of access
to this awareness may itself lead to a secondary experience
of trauma.

In psychoanalytic terms, trauma resides in repetition
and its manifestation in language. A trauma is something
the subject keeps trying not to go back to. Dreams, and
the language used to describe them, find the trauma out –
certain words, continually repeated, become points of focus
around which circulate both the meaning of the dream and
the reality of the trauma. Media images may work in similar
ways, as certain pictures are repeated until they become
the principal signifier of a given situation: school
photographs of abducted and murdered children, images
of the suffocating Liverpool fans pressed against the fence

at the Hillsborough football stadium in Sheffield in 1989, the quasi-biblical famine imagery accompanying reports from Ethiopia in 1984. These images are used initially to support an account of a traumatic event, and then, as they are repeated, to direct its meaning.

The power of images to interpret events and emotions is a basic premiss of art. Throughout history there have been moments when art and society have come together, significantly at moments of catastrophe. Great works such as Géricault's *The Raft of the Medusa*, 1819 or Picasso's *Guernica*, 1937 may be seen as instances of art intervening in social crisis, helping contemporary viewers to contemplate tragedy and understand its meaning. Their success as art lies not so much in the creation of beauty from horror or order from chaos, but rather in the provision of a space in which to think about the events they describe, an image within which meaning may begin to collect.

Both these paintings chart the conversion of a moment of traumatic experience into a landmark in collective memory, though the two artists use different strategies. Géricault builds relationships between the viewer and the shipwrecked individuals on the abandoned raft – we strain forwards with the flag waver, as desperate as he is to attract the attention of the unheeding ship on the horizon; and we are moved by the despair of the father in the foreground, hunched over the body of his son. Picasso opts instead for emblems of universal suffering distilled from the tribulations of the inhabitants of the bombarded town Guernica – images of supplication, disbelief, mourning and death are revealed in harsh light against severely geometric planes of black and grey. Neither artist attempts to document the traumatic event itself, both concentrating instead on its aftermath.

More recently, Andy Warhol worked meaningfully with trauma and its impact both in the lives of individuals and in the media. Warhol was, as Thomas Crow has written in his essay on Warhol in *Modern Art and the Common Culture* (Yale University Press, 1996, p.60), 'attracted to the open sores in American political life' and the repetition prevalent in his work of the early 60s has been described in terms of a compulsion, the affect of a shocked subject. His disaster series of the time documents individual death, mass disruption and state-sponsored murder in a sequence of recycled and repeated imagery of car crashes, national disasters, riots and electric chairs, which cuts straight to the heart of the American psyche.

Contemporary art is no less engaged with society, and is no less appropriate a medium through which to think about trauma. This present publication brings together recent work occupying the territory of trauma. The artists included engage with the subject for a variety of reasons and in a range of different ways. The works encourage contemplation and may perhaps lead to a deeper understanding of the complex situation of trauma in contemporary life. For many of the artists involved, trauma is one of the key sites on which collective identity is established – only in moments of true crisis do we come together – as well as an important manifestation of the relationship between individual action and collective impact.

Using both visual and verbal means of communication, several of the works explore image and language, two key concepts in the function of trauma, and its apprehension. Particularly in a highly mediated environment, the image frequently functions as a non-linguistic reference, a trigger to recall the complex, wide-ranging implications and reverberations of the trauma once it has been subsumed into experience. Paradoxically, language is, however, often the first victim of the traumatic incident, which is often said to leave the victim 'speechless'. The most extreme experiences, whether involving physical or emotional pain, are commonly found to be difficult to recall in detail, often the vague circumstance of their occurrence being the only thing to survive in memory. Victims and witnesses of a trauma frequently find both the incident and its ramifications almost impossible to convey. The impact defies language; a factor evident in both complete breakdown and the shock imparted by simplified, straightforward discussion.

The operation of image and language is a subject of Tracey Moffat's work. Her series of photographic lithographs *Scarred for Life II*, 1999 (pp.54 – 57) combines images with captions, each including a date referring to the time of the incident depicted. The texts' matter-of-fact description contrasts with the evocative quality of the images, which can only suggest the full picture. The situations depicted tend to be domestic and small-scale, but are nonetheless meaningful for those involved, and all the more shocking for their occurrence in the perceived realm of safety that is the home.

Martin Boyce is also involved with the intrusion of the external into the sanctuary of the home, inserting objects and inferences signalling distant disaster into icons of apparent normality. His works focus on the division between the ordered and the chaotic, the controlled and the dangerously anarchic. In *Something's Got to Give*, 1995 (p.12), one of several works to deal with the contrast between real and mediated encounters, the screen-printed text reads, 'Watching all the day's horrors on the evening news, I thought back to earlier and the stuffed toy animal I had seen stuck to the rear window of the car in front of me', a recollection of the uncomfortable need for the normal to co-exist with the extraordinary.

Willie Doherty also works with information that usually comes to us via the media, but his double screen video *Tell Me What You Want*, 1996 (pp.16–17) makes the point that all news material is someone's direct experience: 'I never thought that it would happen to me. You know how it is… It's always someone else. Someone you don't know', while his still photography tends to force an awareness of how what is excluded from such accounts can be as significant as what is included.

Johann Grimonprez's *dial H-I-S-T-O-R-Y*, 1997 (pp.36–39) is an hour-long compilation of aeroplane hijack TV news footage, which moves backwards and forwards between the singular and the collective as the experiences of individuals are gathered together and mediated for the many. Some of the images may be familiar, and take us back to the situation in which we first saw them. Much of the film deals with extreme violence, the degradation and destruction of real people, which we cannot but watch with horrified fascination. The compulsion to continue watching is manipulated in Grimonprez's soundtrack, where it is linked into a kind of universal death drive, given resonance by quotations from Don DeLillo's *White Noise*, a novel intimately concerned with the individual's fear of and fascination with death: 'Shouldn't death be a swan dive, graceful, white-winged and smooth, leaving the surface undisturbed?'.

These works share a use of very specific material, which is enlarged and expanded beyond its immediate context to form associations with the present and future ideas and experience of the viewer. While they demand engagement on a level of recognition, they also trigger the imagination: we may be familiar with the actual events or situations represented in the works, but they do not necessarily come from our own direct experience.

The imaginative leap required to understand another individual's experience of trauma is one of the subjects of Anri Sala's short film *Nocturnes*, 1999 (pp.67–69). In it, we see no violent imagery, only a man tending an aquarium of tropical fish and a second man playing nervously with his hands as he discusses the difficulty he is having readjusting to normal life after several years as a soldier for the United Nations forces. The ex-soldier speaks in confessional mode – he cannot stop re-living the experience of killing people, and he needs us, both film maker and viewer, first to believe in his crimes then absolve him of them. As he talks, the impact of his experience on his identity comes into focus – 'It eats away at your life'.

Language is the tool of Tracey Moffat, Maria Lindberg and Christopher Wool. Lindberg's drawings hover between humour and horror, and use the often hidden implications of language to probe collective memory. Hers is the language of the dream – her captions describe her drawings allusively, as one might a dream, each individual word redirecting and refining the meaning of the image. The drawings operate in the present, yet they often refer to a fearfully remembered past or dreaded future. They articulate a state of mind conditioned by something that might have just happened or may yet.

Wool's text painting *Untitled*, 1991 (pp.80–81), on the other hand, describes a situation that, once suggested, inevitably always will happen. In this painting and in the collaborative work using the same text he made with Felix Gonzalez-Torres, the artist drives the caesura of trauma right into the centre of a familiar situation, hijacking the imagined scenario and locking its protagonists into an interminably circular nightmare, which they can never leave: 'The show is over. The audience gets up to leave. Time to collect their coats and go home. They turn around. No more coats and no more home'. Wool has his audience perpetually turning around, looking behind them for the inescapable fact of trauma. They don't know what it is, but it is there, lodged in the memory, something from which they keep trying to divert their attention.

The futility of such diversion is built into the form and content of Felix Gonzalez-Torres' *"Untitled" (We Don't Remember)*, 1991 (p.33). A stack of sheets of paper with these words printed on them in German, the work is an exhortation to forget. The use of the German language evokes the wartime horrors that continue to be associated with the German nation, and the insistence that they should not be forgotten. Yet the piece is, in fact, an invitation to remember – the viewer is encouraged to take one of the printed sheets home, as a souvenir.

Memory and repetition are key components in the thematics of trauma, and both are at play in Kendell Geers' installation *Double Time*, 2000 (pp.24 – 25). The artist uses found film footage to confront the viewer with the individual's drive towards self-preservation. He loops a short segment from the film *Papillon* showing Steve McQueen doing press-ups in a cell into an endless cycle of effort, accompanied by the actor's repeated assertion, 'I'm gonna be fine'. The work does not allow for a future – we know that he is never, in fact, going to be fine – rather, it provides a space for the staging and re-staging of a traumatic encounter.

Ann-Sofi Sidén's film *QM, I think I call her QM*, 1997 (pp.72 – 75) is also about the provision of a space for the affect of trauma on the mind of the individual. Her film is made under the sign of the Golem, a figure from Jewish folklore, an effigy fashioned from clay and water with spells. It is a powerful but clumsy creature, ready to undertake work and protect its creator from any threatening enemy. Sidén's film describes the descent into madness of a lonely New York psychiatrist who finds, or imagines, the 'Queen of Mud' beneath her bed. She keeps the creature under observation and documents its habits. Her treatment of the Queen of Mud, and her musings about it, reveal much about the psychiatrist's own state of mind – the creature, the room in which she is incarcerated and the house into which the psychiatrist progressively barricades herself in the course of the film all provide a space in which to explore psychological damage.

Sidén's work is based on real-life material the artist found in a house in New York, and it tells a specific narrative. Yet the aura and atmosphere it creates stay with you long after you have finished watching it, imbuing other actions, objects and situations with a particular sense of unease. This power to sensitize is shared by all the artists in this publication, whether, like Sidén or Sala, their works tell the story of a particular individual or whether, like Lindberg's drawings or Lucia Nogueira's troubling, enigmatic objects, they set the

stage for as yet uncomprehended events. Nogueira's *Slip*, 1992 (p.61) and *Compass*, 1993 (pp.62 – 63), one a chipped bell jar set on a glass plinth, the other a wire structure half wrenched off the wall, seem to stand in for the threatened or traumatized individual. Whether prelude or aftermath, we are not sure, but it seems clear that these objects are linked to the disruption of the norm.

Nogueira's objects collect together meaning, both intended by the artist and brought to the work by the viewer. They seem to reflect or describe a situation, but also to precipitate it. Meaning circulates around them, yet they also bring the viewer up short in front of them, making a gap in experience, which mimics the operation of trauma. This artist's work is allusive, its effect subtle in comparison with some of the other more directly traumatic or traumatized work.

The artists whose work is presented here develop a range of different relationships with trauma in which they in turn involve the viewer to varying degrees. Some place themselves and the viewer in the position of witness to a particular event and its potential or actual aftermath. Others generate a situation for the potential of trauma within the work itself. Few draw on personal experience: they are not concerned with art as therapy or exorcism in a direct way. Rather, through mediating the issue through a range of different modes, they offer the viewer the chance to contemplate it as an intrinsic part of the experience of living, and as subject matter for a significant strand within contemporary art. As art takes account of life, so it addresses trauma, making spaces for its consideration which are memorable, meaningful and often moving.

Martin Boyce

Born 1967, Glasgow, Scotland
Lives and works in Glasgow

Reference
Martin Boyce, Fruitmarket Gallery,
Edinburgh, 2000

Martin Boyce works with images and objects from the history of design, film and architecture that have somehow become of broader cultural significance. In recent years, he has often used classic modernist design objects, in particular items designed in the 1940s and 50s by the renowned American partnership of Charles and Ray Eames. Boyce exploits the ability of such objects to recall the ethos of the time of their creation – a moment when the pursuit of perfectly ordered, simple and efficient living space prevailed. The belief that quality of life could be enhanced by the creation of better and better commodities, through the deployment of innovative materials and technologies, was the guiding force behind much of the modernist project.

The atmosphere of anxiety and even paranoia that pervades Boyce's works highlights the failure of these idealistic projects truly to deliver a better, brighter new world. His work also emphasizes the friction generated by our on-going quest for a clean, safe, ordered and transparent society and the reality of a disordered, even aggressive, urban environment.

The objects, drawings and photographs of his recent works are rooted in recognizable forms, but are imbued with evidence or the suggestion of an aggressive incident. The objects present are somehow altered, rendered useless and stripped of their potential to offer order. Deprived of their perfect form, these are objects whose function is frustrated, whose rational existence has been annihilated by events.

Now I've Got Worry (Storage Unit), 1997 (p.13) is an Eames shelving unit re-made by the artist in which some of the brightly coloured Formica panels have been replaced with makeshift signs found in the urban environment. The boards, each bearing defensive messages ('PRIVATE PROPERTY – KEEP OUT' and 'GO HOME – THERE IS NOTHING 2 SEE'), speak of personal space invaded and encroached upon by an undesirable outside world. One can only guess at a reason for their creation, but they are undoubtedly the result of some kind of breakdown, which has caused the author to seek seclusion.* Boyce has described the piece as 'part shelving unit reconstructed using signs ripped from empty back lots, part architectural model and part three-dimensional Mondrian'. Like so much of his recent work, it evokes an intense sense of darkness and disorder as it impinges on our ordered, sanitized urban environments.

At the heart of each of Boyce's works lies a traumatic encounter, whether physical, psychological or both. They express the unhappy collision between the domestic interior and the urban exterior, between order and chaos, protection and aggression, between the dream and the nightmare.
KB

*'The front of the alleyway in which the bodies of Nicole Brown Simpson and Ronald Lyle Goldman were found has been screened off by a dozen or so dwarf maples still inside their black PVC nursery tubs. It is further hidden by previous plantings of Australian tree ferns and Nile lilies behind a new enclosure of green-plasticated chain-link fence that separates the walkway from the sidewalk (this part of Brentwood has sidewalks).

Signs put up by agitated neighbours saying "GET A LIFE" and "GO HOME THERE IS NOTHING 2 SEE" have been taken down. By August 4, late afternoon traffic no longer concertinas to a grind the way it did in the initial sensationalist frenzy of a few weeks ago. But it still slows down.'
(Douglas Coupland, 'The Brentwood Notebook' in *Polaroids from the Dead*, Flamingo, London, 1996, p.174)

watching all the day's horrors on the evening news, I
thought back to earlier and the stuffed toy animal I had
seen stuck to the rear window of the car in front of me

2
Now I've Got Worry
(Storage Unit)
1997

Willie
Doherty

Born 1959, Derry, Northern Ireland
Lives and works in Derry

References
Willie Doherty: Somewhere Else, Tate Gallery
Liverpool, 1998
Willie Doherty; same old story, Matt's Gallery,
London; Firstsite, Colchester; Orchard Gallery,
Derry, 1997

Even the most apparently innocent of Willie Doherty's photographs is imbued with a deep sense of rupture, of the aftermath of consequential and malicious incident. His eerily still images provoke an acute awareness that we are being asked to examine a place somehow altered or affected by recent events. Many of his best-known photographic works provide quite distinct evidence of incident: burned-out cars, barricaded roads. Yet the viewer is always prevented from achieving an absolute, rationalized reading of the situation depicted – the camera angle is too tight, the crucial information we seek to complete the picture seems eternally just outside the field of vision to which we are given access. Was what we see occasioned by accident or intent? In Doherty's images, our view is only ever partial. If only we could see the whole picture.

Such deliberate frustration of our desire to read and therefore to understand lies at the heart of Doherty's practice. His works with still photography and video share a concern with perspective, with the position from which our understanding is construed. Rooted in the deeply divided and contested arena that is Northern Ireland, Doherty's work expands on this context to explore globally significant issues of subjectivity. His focus is on the highly coded and mediated nature of our interface with our surroundings.

The spaces and places recorded by Doherty's camera and the atmospheres they evoke speak ineffably of trauma. These images, devoid of human presence, are nonetheless rich in its trace. Whether offering a vision of damage – *Abandoned Interior II* and *III*, 1997 (pp.18–19) – or contaminated space – *Out of Sight*, 1997 (p.20) – they record or suggest the results of aggressive encounters. The body is absent but the forms, materials and impressions of the objects present in each image makes its imminence felt. What the spaces depicted have in common is that they are peripheral, marginal areas where order has subsided or been over-ridden by active disorder.

An eschewal of the single, authoritative viewpoint is apparent in the double perspective employed in the video installation *Tell Me What You Want*, 1996 (pp.16–17). This piece shares with many of Doherty's other works a concern with the impact that events have on the lives of those they touch. It focuses on the way one event reverberates through the community in which it unfolds. The piece is shown on two monitors, positioned opposite each other. One begins with a close-up shot of a rain-drenched road at night, the only light the reflected glow of streetlights, while the other shows a similarly close view of a road-side grassy verge in daylight, accompanied by the sound of birds. These images soon give way to blacked-out head shots of a man and a woman, their faces obscured in the style familiar from TV crime documentary. Each proceeds to recount their views of a recent incident, re-assessing their actions and thoughts in the light of what they now know: '[…] I never thought he would do that. […] I had no idea that there was someone listening to me…watching me. […] I never thought that it would happen to me. […] I didn't recognise him at the time, but I found out later who he was', and so on. The incident itself is never explained or recounted in full – we are party only to these reflections on the aftermath.
KB

Man: …I never thought that it would happen to me. You know how it is…it's always someone else. Someone you don't know.

…She didn't look like the sort of woman who would be involved in that kind of thing, was very quiet, kept herself to herself. I couldn't believe it when I heard she was dead. It was like a dream.

…As soon as I saw him I knew he was one of them. He had a certain look on his face. After that he was a fucking dead man.

…I hate walking alone in the country. I feel exposed and vulnerable. I keep thinking someone is watching me or following me and I can't see them. I'm also frightened that I might find a body that has been hidden in the bushes.

…One night I had a dream that I was taken prisoner. I was blindfolded and held in a small room. I lost all track of time. I don't know how long I was in there. Eventually three men came into the room. They tied me to a chair and asked me questions about my life. I thought they were going to kill me.

…I didn't know what was happening at the time. Like everyone else I read the newspaper reports and saw it on TV. As soon as I saw the body lying in the grass I knew it was her…I recognised the pattern of her jumper.

…I knew there was something going on even though no-one was talking about it. I could smell trouble…I could feel the tension. I wanted to find clues…I went looking for evidence. Look! The photographs prove everything.

…I never thought that it would happen to me. You know how it is…it's always someone else. Someone you don't know…

Woman: The first time I met him was in 1989. I thought he was OK but a little crazy sometimes. But I never thought he would do that.

…You hear all kinds of stories about people being watched and their house being bugged. I never really believed it, to tell you the truth… I wasn't even suspicious. I never heard any noise, never saw anything. I had no idea that there was someone listening to me …watching me.

…I never thought it would happen to me. You know how it is…It's always someone else. Someone you don't know…

…Well, I was just walking down the street when I suddenly saw this guy being led away by a bunch of cops. I didn't recognise him at the time, but I found out later who he was.

…She didn't look like the sort of woman who would be involved in that kind of thing, was very quiet, kept herself to herself. I couldn't believe it when I heard she was dead. It was like a dream.

…I hate walking alone in the country. I feel exposed and vulnerable. I keep thinking someone is watching me or following me…and I can't see them. I'm also frightened that I might find a body that has been hidden in the bushes.

…Her body was found dumped on the track near the border by a woman out walking at 7am. Several hours earlier there had been reports of shots being heard in the area.

…The first time I met him was in 1989. I thought he was OK but a little crazy sometimes. But I never thought he would do that.

4
Abandoned Interior II
1997

Kendell Geers

Born May 1968
Lives and works in London, England; Leipzig,
Germany; Vienna, Austria; and *Alphaville*

References
Christine Macel, 'Kendell Geers. Porcelain
and Volcano', *Kendell Geers*, Secession,
Vienna, 1999
Okwui Enwezor, 'Altered States: The Art of
Kendell Geers', 1997, www.kendell-geers.net

Kendell Geers' work is characterized by violence, fragmentation and fracture. His art sets up situations in which artist, viewer and protagonist might be placed at risk, and seeks to undermine confidence in the unified nature of experience.

The artist's interest in fragmentation begins with his own identity. His place and date of birth are fictitious, chosen to coincide with both the French student uprisings and the death of Marcel Duchamp. His refusal to be categorized in terms either of generation or geography extends also to his current place of residence, and to his politics – *Untitled (ANC, AVF, AWB, CP, DP, IFP, PAC, SACP)*, 1993–94 involved him simultaneously joining all the political parties of his native South Africa, a move that led to a consideration of the precarious nature of social and political identity, while also making the artist vulnerable to considerable personal danger. A sense of impending or actual physical harm runs throughout his work, damage to the material body a trope through which ideas of mental and conceptual disintegration may be explored.

Cry Wolf, 1999 (pp.26–27) is a pile of red emergency lights jumbled on the floor. Seductive in the beauty of their form, they nevertheless signal distress and damage. The lights operate in the realm of the familiar – we all have visual references for them, have seen them in the street, in films and on TV. Out of context and aestheticized, their meaning remains rather worryingly intact; as the artist states, 'it has never been about the found object, but rather about evoking a sense of danger, an explosion of energy directed towards the complete implosion of language, that moment where it all falls apart'. Falling apart characterizes the artist's attitude to materials as well as meanings – his sculpture is complemented by work with film and video, which loop recognizable fragments of film together in such a way as to dissect our experience of common culture as well as the work itself.

The beauty of *Cry Wolf* is crucial to its operation as art. The appeal it exerts is a kind of fascination, perhaps a horrified fascination – both an emotional and visceral response to the urgency of the flashing red lights. At the same time as drawing the viewer towards it, the work also threatens the viewer, first conceptually, as it makes us consider the situations in which all its lights may come into use, and also physically, there in the gallery. The work is hard to look at – it is too bright, it may make us blink and recoil, the safety of our body compromised.

The operation of threat in the meaning of *Cry Wolf* works against the recognition with which the sculpture also plays. In much of his work, Geers tends to use recognition to draw the viewer in, holding out a promise of completion which he then undermines. *Double Time*, 2000 (pp.24–25) is an installation with two video monitors mounted on scaffolding. The monitors are domestic TVs, the scaffolding rusty and well-used, the film footage familiar. All the signs are that we will be comfortable with this work, able to slot it easily into our experience. However, this is not the case. The film loop shows the actor Steve McQueen playing the role of a man trying to hold it all together. Over and over he completes a press-up, rising into the frame then dipping back down, muttering the same phrase like a mantra – '…I'm gonna be fine…I'm gonna be fine…'. The work collapses past and future into a nightmarish present: we remember the film; its protagonist is preparing for the future, yet both he and we, as we become mesmerized by him, are locked into the circulatory space of an individual trying to remain intact in the face of a nameless threat.
FB

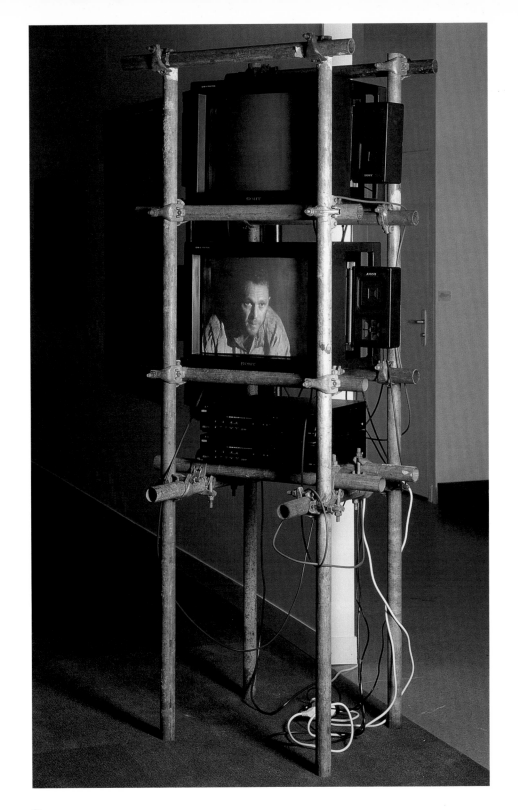

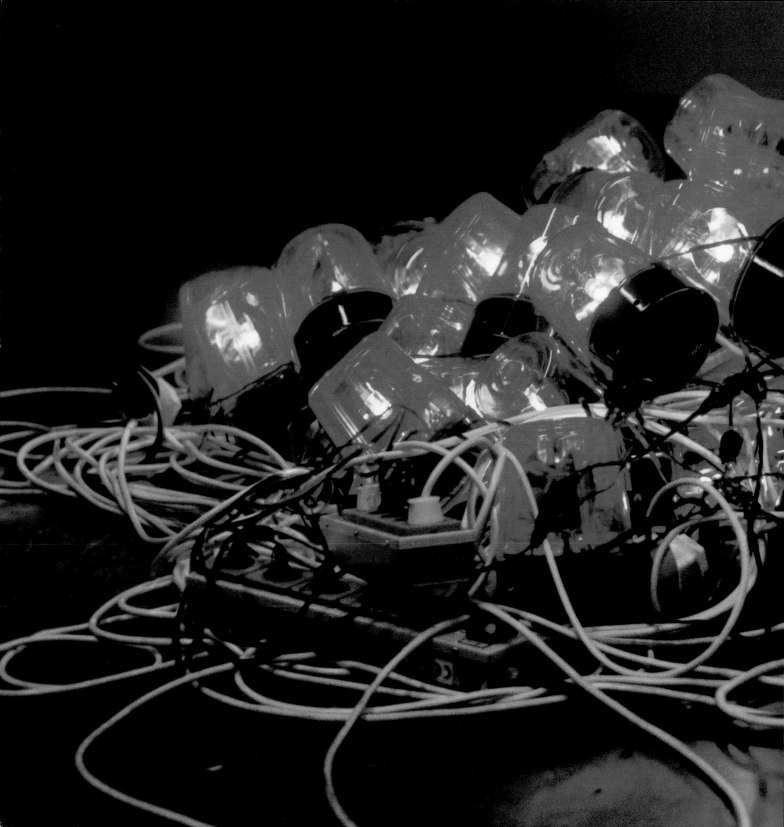

Felix
Gonzalez-Torres

Born 1957, Guäimaro, Cuba
Lived and worked in New York, USA from 1979
Died 1996, Miami, USA

References
Felix Gonzalez-Torres, A.R.T. Press,
Los Angeles, 1993
Nancy Spector, *Felix Gonzalez-Torres*,
Guggenheim Museum, New York, 1995

Using simple, often industrially-produced materials while subverting the formal vocabulary of minimalism, Felix Gonzalez-Torres developed a body of work that negotiates complex and resonant issues, among them the individual's relation to the social, the private to the public. Exploiting the evocative potential of words, colour and images, his work elucidates a range of human experiences and emotions including fear, loss, desire, an awareness of mortality, and the potential for immortality. His interest in the function of memory pervades his work, which frequently conjures a sense of temporal shift or disjunction, of transportation to another place or time.

Gonzalez-Torres is best known for his works that allow the viewer to take something with them as they leave the place of exhibition: his paper stacks and 'candy spills', piles of wrapped sweets from which the viewer may remove and even consume one. Of these works, Gonzalez-Torres said, 'Without a public these works are nothing, nothing'. Forcing a consideration of just where the boundary between artwork and viewer might lie, if it exists at all, these works are the epitome of his perpetual concern with fragmentation and dispersal.

Combining his own personal experiences and memories with an incisive engagement with issues of collective or shared perspective, Gonzalez-Torres' work often make use of reduced, simple text to evoke meaningful people, places and experiences. The absence of image in these works should not, however, be construed as a denial of the power of the image. It is rather an acknowledgement of our dependency on images, particularly the photographic, to recall sensations of past experiences. The works function in full awareness of our habitual reliance on the image of somewhere or someone special, of the photograph as souvenir. Gonzalez-Torres' insistence in these text-based works on depriving us of the photograph's power to transport the viewer to another time and place is fundamental to his interest in memory.

Gonzalez-Torres' 'portraits', begun in the late 1980s, use just a few lines of text to capture something of their subject – a list of people and events, each followed by a year, which suggests something of the life experience of the person 'depicted'. Avoiding literal description, these lists imply incidents – personal and private encounters, radical cultural shifts and international news stories – all of which have variously impacted on and resonate through the individual's memory. They are the events that have shaped that personality, which have allowed the development of a unique identity. Our responses to the lists suggest both the power and the fragility of collective memory in a global culture – some may be familiar and significant to everyone while others are marginal or even unknown. That these portraits are presented as small, delicate photostats, their own probable disintegration all too apparent, serves only to enhance the possibility that the subject and all its associations may disappear from memory.

Another work, a stack of paper – *"Untitled" (We Don't Remember)*, 1991 (p.33) – bears the German phrase 'Wir erinnern uns nicht' (We don't remember) contained in a bold red rectangle centred on each printed sheet. The insistence that 'We don't remember' wears thin, as the words appear over and over again on each new sheet revealed by the removal of the topmost, the phrase running like a stain throughout the piece. Is this an inability to remember or a refusal? The phrase in German is more ambiguous than the English, leaving us wondering if it is indeed only by constant repetition of the phrase that the events are not to be brought back to mind. Endless recurrence of the phrase seems only to amplify the significance of the unknown incident, while the insistent 'We' coupled with the gradual dispersal of the sheets forces the act of not remembering into the domain of collective memory and response.
KB

Patty Hearst 1975 Jaws 1975 Vietnam
1975 Watergate 1973 Bruce Lee 1973
Munich 1972 Waterbeds 1971 Jackie 1968

12
"Untitled" (We Don't Remember)
1991

Johan
Grimonprez

Born 1962, Roeselare, Trinidad
Lives and works in New York, USA
and Ghent, Belgium

Reference
Catherine Bernard, 'Supermarket History',
Parkett, no. 53, Zürich/New York, 1998

Simply described, *dial H-I-S-T-O-R-Y*, 1997 (pp.36–39) is a seventy minute long collage of television and film clippings, old and new, that appear to document in a disjointed way the history of aeroplane hijackings. The sound is also a mix: of newsreel reports, excerpts from the American writer Don DeLillo's books *White Noise* and *Mao II* and 1970s classic soul and funk tracks. But no description can prepare the viewer for the visual and intellectual richness of Johan Grimonprez's film. Shown to international acclaim at *Documenta X* in Kassel, Germany, in 1997, *dial H-I-S-T-O-R-Y* is arguably one of the defining works of art created in recent years.

Grimonprez's overriding subject is how the media participates in the construction of reality. Through seeing extracts from original TV reports of hijacks and their aftermath, the viewer of *dial H-I-S-T-O-R-Y* experiences the voyeurism of news reporting during a traumatic event, in which everything is given a meaning according to a particular agenda:
'*press conference*
– The airplane is safe.
– Tell me. There has been a report that the hijacker had asked for some sandwiches. Did he get those sandwiches?
– No, sir.'

The title of the work and the way in which it flicks between different film footage – from the above exchange at Rome airport to film of Lenin, from Malcolm X to a hijack in Fukuoka, Japan – suggests history is there to be played with, formulated at will, even that there is too much history. How do we choose from all this material what is important and should be remembered and what should be forgotten? The era of the individual hijacker, such as the idealistic Leila Khaled, whose name we would have once known, is over and their stories are forgotten. But Grimonprez's film places hijacking not at the margins but at the centre of how we might construct recent history with its contested ideologies and disputed territories. He reminds us of the ambivalent and changing international view of hijacking from something close to admiration (a spate of hijacks to Cuba) to horror at the inhuman brutality of international terrorism, which no amount of revolutionary talk can justify.

In a cool and questioning counterpoise to the seductive thrill of the ride and the upbeat soundtrack music – which is itself at odds with the seriousness of events – a disembodied voice reads extracts from Don DeLillo. There is, it seems, no escape from the media-saturated world:

'Everything around us tends to channel our lives toward some final reality in print or on film. Two lovers quarrel in the back of the taxi and a question becomes implicit in the event. Who will write the book and who will play the lovers in the movie? Everything seeks its own heightened version. Nothing happens until it is consumed.'

In *dial H-I-S-T-O-R-Y*, Grimonprez returns us to the collective trauma of hijack disasters with their hostages and exploding aeroplanes, personal and political intent, public and private grief, deliberate acts and chance encounters. Having only one lens we can look through, instead of significance and understanding we get the absurd and the bluntly horrifying – a dead hostage falls from an aeroplane window, pools of blood are swept up like milk. While offering no solutions, Grimonprez's film is a *tour de force* of rare critical ambition, which reveals with astonishing visual adeptness and force our own complicity in the making of history.
AN

13

(pp. 36–39)
transcript extract
and stills from
dial H-I-S-T-O-R-Y
1997

(p.37)
Design: Peter Stemmler
and Alex Kellas
Photography: Rony Vissers

voice over 1
Shouldn't death be a swan dive, graceful, white-winged and smooth, leaving the surface undisturbed?
titles
dial H-I-S-T-O-R-Y
a film by Johan Grimonprez
press conference
– The airplane is safe.
– Tell me. There had been a report that the hijacker had asked for some sandwiches. Did he get those sandwiches?
– No, sir.
titles
November 1969
FIRST TRANSATLANTIC HIJACK
Vietnam vet Raffaele Minichiello hijacks American airliner back home to Rome.
voice over 2
Everything around us tends to channel our lives toward some final reality in print or on film. Two lovers quarrel in the back of a taxi and a question becomes implicit in the event. Who will write the book and who will play the lovers in the movie? Everything seeks its own heightened version. Nothing happens until it's consumed.
voice over 2
There's the haunted time of the novelist, intimate, stale and sad. Every book is a bug-eyed race, let's face it. Must finish. Can't die yet.
voice over 1
He was often lost. He got lost in the hotel every time he walked out of his room and turned left to get to the elevator, which was consistently to the right.
titles
March 1970, Fukuoka, Japan
JAPANESE RED ARMY SEIZES
AIRLINER WITH SAMURAI SWORDS
titles
Tokyo Streets Deserted:
MILLIONS WATCH
FIRST TELEVISED HIJACK
titles
May 1970
Hiroshima, Japan
voice over 1
All plots tend to move deathwards. This is the nature of plots.

Political plots, terrorist plots, lovers' plots, narrative plots, plots that are part of children's games. We edge nearer death every time we plot. It's like a contract that all must sign, the plotters as well as those who are targets of the plots.
voice over 2
It is a curious knot that binds novelists and terrorists. What terrorists gain, novelists lose. Years ago, I used to think it was possible for a novelist to alter the inner life of the culture. Now, bomb-makers and gunmen have taken that territory. They make raids on human consciousness. What writers used to do before we were all incorporated.
titles
June 1972
Tel Aviv, Israel
KOZO OKAMOTO TRIED FOR LOD AIRPORT MASSACRE
titles
We, Red Army Soldiers wanted to become stars of Orion when we'd die. It calms my heart to think that all of the people we killed will also becomes stars in the same sky. As the revolution goes on, how the stars will multiply – Kozo Okamoto
voice over 1
When he woke up on the hotel bed, he was in shorts, still wearing his socks and one shoe. He'd removed his pants, or someone had, without taking off his left shoe. Rides to airports made him quiet and glum. He listened to news updates on the radio, curiously excited reports about firemen removing a burning sofa from a tenement in Watertown.
titles
STUDY
REVEALS
DOG LOVERS
LIVE LONGER
THAN
CAT LOVERS
titles
Nagoya Airport, Japan
press conference
– Mister Brill, you are back among your family now. How was it like?
– It was a gamut of very many emotions: from surprise to shock, to fear, to joy, to laughter and then again fear at the end, yes and almost tragedy, yes.
(continues…)

Guillermo Kuitca

Born 1961, Buenos Aires, Argentina
Lives and works in Buenos Aires

References
Art from Argentina, Museum of Modern Art, Oxford, 1994
Guillermo Kuitca, Fondation Cartier pour l'art contemporain, Paris, 2000

Guillermo Kuitca's paintings and installations are profound reflections on displacement, loss and memory. The grandson of Ukrainian Jews who settled in Argentina in the early 1900's, Kuitca first came to international attention when he began to paint maps of geographical regions onto mattresses, displayed horizontally on beds or on the wall. In these pieces, the maps appear to stand in for the absent body. The viewer is drawn into exploring the vein-like networks and clusters of coloured lines that represent routes and road systems. In the same way that a map can only tell us certain things about a place, so an object as potentially meaningful as an old mattress is, in Kuitca's art, strangely silent, its power coming from the breadth of its allusions and our own engagement with the work. Influenced by an interest in theatre (before devoting himself to painting he worked as a theatre director) Kuitca's works have the expressive realism and impact of a live performance in which the empty stage is psychologically charged, the tension dependant on both an expectation of action and the audience's own presence.

In the monumental canvas *People on Fire*, 1993 (pp.42–43), Kuitca addresses a subject central to our understanding of the human condition in the twentieth century: how do we come to terms with the trauma of the Holocaust, the missing, the disappeared, all those rubbed out of history? Seeking to make maps of people, rather than of cities, Kuitca has painted a vast genealogical chart. Many of the names have been blocked out, a poignant reference to the large number of people who have disappeared following atrocities perpetrated by the military junta in Argentina. This painting is one of a series of works with the same title, and in all of them the artist selected anonymous families, as if seeking to distance himself from his own involvement and put himself more in the position of the viewer.

While the artist, in one sense, removes himself from the work, his physical trace is present in the application of paint. Kuitca has spoken about how he worked from the centre of the canvas, allowing his body to smear the wet paint and erase whole branches of the family tree.

While the title of the work summons up horrific images from television, old newsreels and first-hand accounts, Kuitca's chart, like his maps, retains a certain objectiveness. The work acts as a catalyst, triggering the viewer's own personal and collective memories, stories and images.

Untitled, 1995 (p.45) depicts, extremely minimally, a theatre stage. In earlier work, Kuitca painted assemblages of set furniture, sometimes with small figures moving among it. Here, however, everything except the stage itself has been obliterated. Sketched onto an expanse of grey, it is as if removed from a specific time and place. The theatre is empty, the back wall blank. The suggestion of the theatre leaves us unsure whether it is waiting for an event or recovering from it. Either way, for Kuitca, the viewer is always a witness not a bystander, responsible to both history and the future.
AN

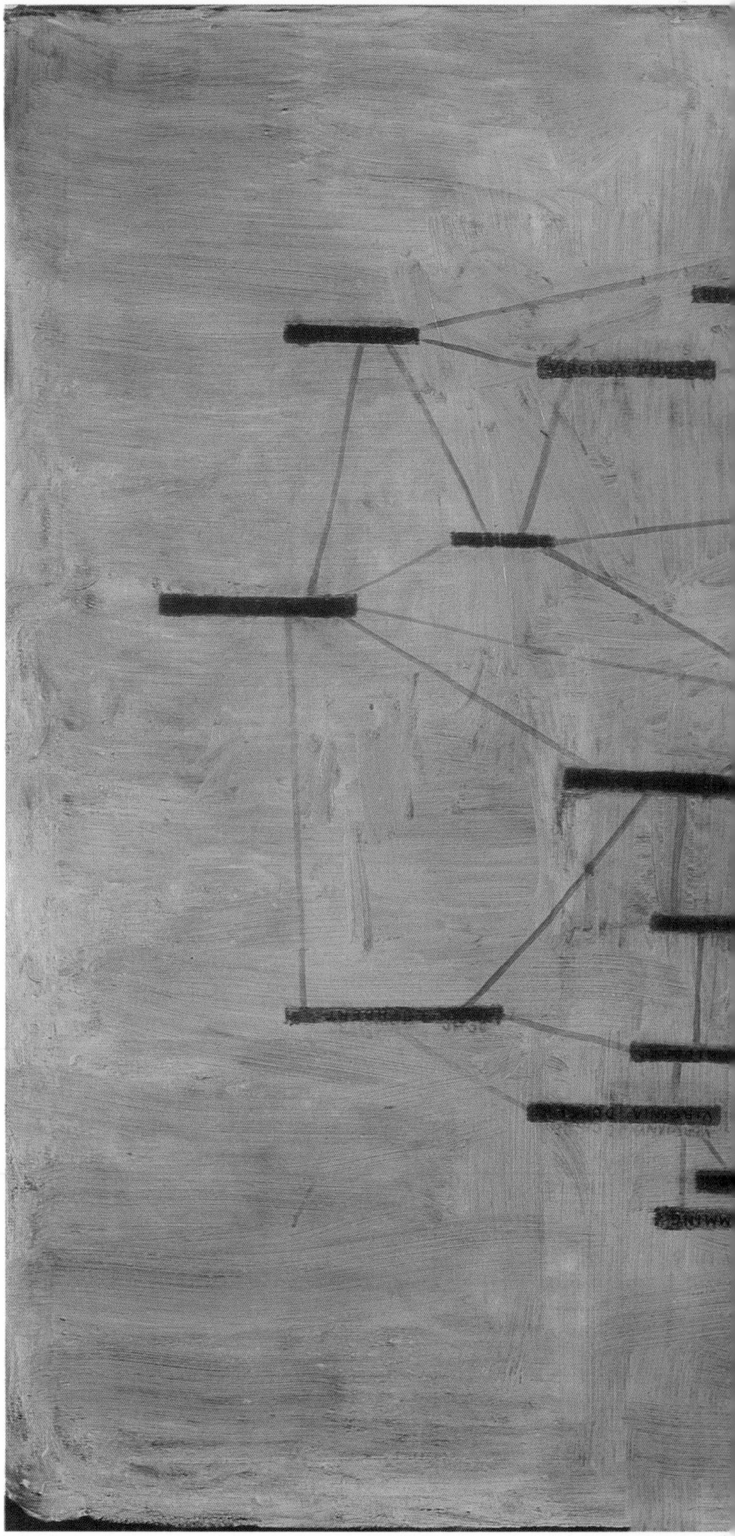

14
People on Fire
1993

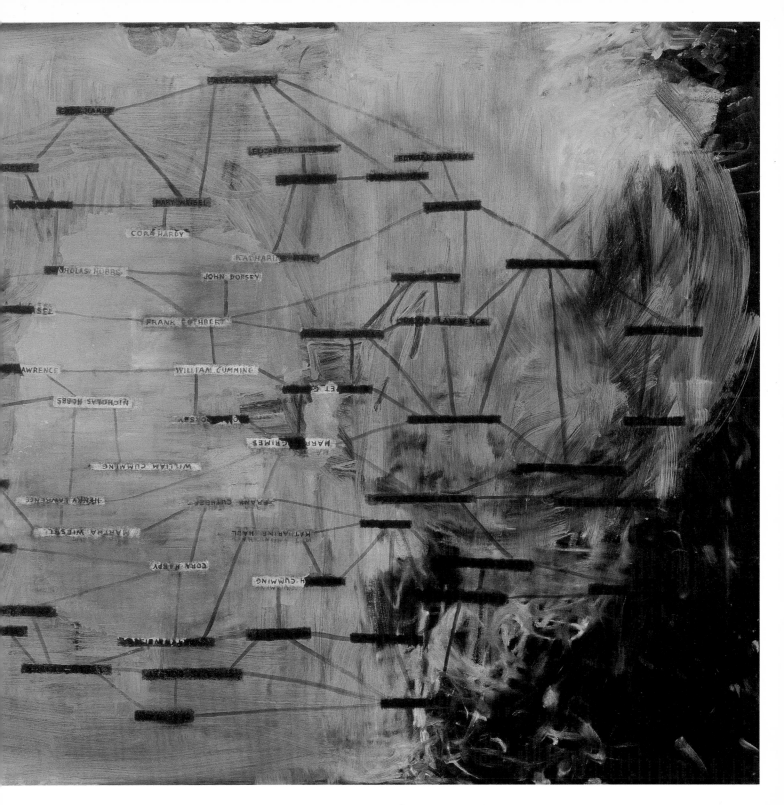

15
Untitled
1995

Maria
Lindberg

Born 1958, Ljushult, Sweden
Lives and works in Stockholm, Sweden

References
Åsa Nacking, *Maria Lindberg*,
Andréhn-Schiptjenko Gallery,
Stockholm, 2000

Maria Lindberg's work has been described by Åsa Nacking in a recent book on the artist as 'an investigation into memory, identity, loneliness, longing, intimacy, fear, sorrow and loss'. Since 1990 she has been concentrating mostly on drawing, making slight, fragile work, which nevertheless packs a powerful punch.

Lindberg believes that form should not dominate content, rather that 'hand and thought are one', and that content should somehow discover its correct form in the process of its artistic expression. Her work is economical in its means – she makes her marks work as hard as those of written language. Conceptually, too, her drawing has similarities with the functioning of language, both in the sense that carefully chosen words are capable simultaneously of expressing and refining thought, and in the way in which one word may be used where at least ten others are inferred. The artist thinks this is particularly true of the English language, and often captions her work with English titles, written directly onto the page as part of the drawing.

Language most obviously demonstrates its capacity for signaling several things at once in metaphoric usage, and much of Lindberg's work is concerned with restoring to language the metaphoric potential that it has lost through over-use – *The First Cut is the Deepest*, 1999; *Pieces of Reality*, 1998; *A Last Glance of You*, 1997. Some of this work borders on the savage, for example, *He Took my Hand*, a work

from 1993, which shows one person's hand coming off in another's. The metaphor here is one of power, and this is an area in which Lindberg operates with particular clarity. Her work often seems to show women ensnared by structures, linguistic and otherwise, over which they have no control: *Girl in Reconstruction*, 1996 shows a woman hedged about by harsh marks while *Double Exposures (Milwaukee)*, 1998 (p.49) is an amusing double-take on domestic expectation ('Honey, I'm home…').

Several of Lindberg's drawings are incomplete, and thus provide a space for ambiguity and reflection on the part of the viewer. One series of works involves drawings that have been partially or completely rubbed out – *Long Ago and Far Away*, 1997 articulates its sense of loss and loneliness through faintness, so that we have to strain to see the house in the drawing as though it has been obscured by time or distance rather than the operation of the eraser. *Lost Friend*, 1996 works in a similar way, the tenuous marks of the woman's face indicating both physical and psychological withdrawal.

The notion of time passing, and the sense that our experience of the present moment is unstable, even untrustworthy, is accentuated in the drawing *Minutes Ago*, 1999 (pp.50 – 51). A large, red number five, floating in solitary splendour on a blank background, the drawing seems to know something we don't. It articulates a state of mind conditioned by something unknown that has just

happened and again, it seems to have something to do with power play – the idea that someone, somewhere knows more than we do. Things that may have just happened or that may yet, or that may be going on right now but just not here, these are all factors in the particular situation of unease that several of Lindberg's drawings set up. A recent sound work compounds this. Called *As Above So Below*, 2000, it consists of a microphone placed in one space and a loudspeaker in another. The microphone records the sound of footsteps walking in the distant space and relays it to the viewer via the loudspeaker. Lindberg tends to place the work in spaces where the floors are made of different materials, so that the speaker plays sounds that could not possibly be made in the room in which it and the viewer currently are. The effect is subtle, but undeniably spooky.

Lindberg's drawings are, for the most part, simple. Pinned directly on the wall, they have a homely quality often at odds with the casual savagery or sadness of their subject matter. Their appeal is direct and material – unframed and unprotected, they have a definite physicality. They are vulnerable, and some, like people, bear the marks of their history upon them. Lindberg is aware of their fragility as objects, and of the metaphorical implications of this. *Abused Drawing*, 1995 – 99 (p.48), hovering as it does between humour and horror, makes this clear.
FB

Abused drawing

24
Double Exposures (Milwaukee)
1998

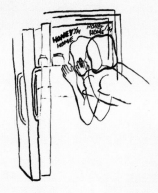

minutes ago

Tracey Moffatt

Born 1960, Brisbane, Australia
Lives and works in Sydney, Australia
and New York, USA

References
Adrian Martin, 'The Go-Between',
World AA Magazine, Melbourne, 1995,
no.2, pp.22–29
Tom McEuilley, 'Falling Upward',
Interview Magazine, New York, April 1998
Regis Durand, *Specific Climates*,
Fundacio La Caixa, Barcelona, 1999

In *Something More*, 1989, Tracey Moffatt's sequence of photographic images, identity, race, gender, violence and the erotic all jostle for attention in what appear to be Hollywood movie stills. Set in the Australian outback, each 'frame' is brimming with possible narratives. There is not one story but hybrids of many.

Aboriginal by birth but brought up by white parents, Moffatt's work almost revels in the contradictions of cultural difference and confused identity. The contrast between the melodramatic and comic juxtapositions in her images and the seriousness of the issues at stake reveal the reality of 'mixed' emotions and conflicting aspirations, which runs through her work. Drawing on her own memories but adopting the style and look of visual motifs from television, movies and popular culture, Moffatt's work is both specific to an Australian context and yet universal in its commentary on the search for social affirmation.

The images in *Scarred for Life II*, 1999 (pp.54–57) follow the same format as a previous series made in 1994. In them both, Moffatt pastiches the documentary image and text story style to be found in post-war mass circulation magazines such as *Life*. Each image is dated as if one of a sequence specific to that particular person. In the earlier series, Moffatt moves with unnerving ease from the traumatic incident to the absurd: 'Birth Certificate, 1962. During the fight, her mother threw her birth certificate at her. This is how she found out her real father's name.' 'Doll Birth, 1972. His mother caught him giving birth to a doll. He was banned from playing with the boy next door again.'

In the first of the above pieces, an Aboriginal woman in her nightdress is squatting down beside a bathroom sink. She leans against the side of the sink, her head on her arm. She holds the certificate between her hands. She stares out towards us with an exhausted but questioning look as if we have stumbled into the scene.

In *Scarred for Life II*, Moffatt has created a further ten scenes with even more emphasis on the surreal and absurd:

'Scissor Cut, 1980. For punishment the Kwong sisters were forced to cut the front lawn with scissors.' 'Pantyhose Arrest, 1973. For his own safety while he played, his mother tied him up with pantyhose. The next-door neighbours called the police.'

The matter-of-fact images seem to show what is said in the captions and vice versa. Moffatt dramatizes what appear to be dysfunctional or abusive relationships and the way in which the apparently trivial may become traumatic. But she does not allow us to make a 'correct' interpretation or simple judgement regarding these situations. Rather, the experience of looking at Moffatt's work is one of endlessly searching, moving from one provocative signpost to another. The viewer's gaze is not frustrated but stimulated by Moffatt's engaging re-evaluation of social codes and the roles they play in repressing or promoting identity and expression.
AN

Tracey Moffatt

Pantyhose Arrest, 1973

For his own safety while he played, his mother tied him up with pantyhose.
The next-door neighbours called the police.

Homemade Hand-knit, 1958

He knew his team mates were chuckling over
his mother's hand-knitted rugby uniform.

Tracey Moffatt

Scissor Cut, 1980

For punishment the Kwong sisters were
forced to cut the front lawn with scissors.

Tracey Moffatt

Piss Bags, 1978

Locked in the van while their mothers continued their affair,
the boys were forced to piss into their chip bags.

Tracey Moffatt

57

Lucia Nogueira

Born 1950, Goiania, Brazil
Lived and worked in London, England from 1975
Died 1998, London, England

References
Anthony Downey, Rainer Fuchs,
Lucia Nogueira, Galerie Eugen Lendl, 1997
Andrew Wilson, *Lucia Nogueira*,
Ikon Gallery, 1993

The strength of Lucia Nogueira's work lies in its ability to be both seductive and threatening. We are drawn to its poetry and beauty but the evidence of our eyes also leaves us unsettled. Attracting the viewer's gaze with an acute sensitivity to materials and media, Nogueira's works are unstable, highly-charged 'landscapes' that are as much about elsewhere and displacement, the past and the future, as about immediate experience. Are we witnesses to the aftermath of a traumatic occurrence, or is something still to happen?

Compass, 1993 (pp.62–63) is a rectangular metal structure covered in black wax, screwed to the wall. Seen in a gallery, we are sensitized to the fact of its creation as art, yet its aesthetic properties are also those that make it an assertive and problematic construction. Its form is both elegant and potentially horrifying. In one corner there is a single unwaxed metal end, sharpened to a deadly point.

The purpose of a compass is to establish your location relative to magnetic north, a fixed position. By calling the piece 'compass', Nogueira surely suggests more than a formal association. A work of art can give the viewer new perceptions, new bearings. The metal point ruptures contemplative reverie or silence, lifting the lid on worlds far removed from issues of formal innovation or artistic currency.

Born in Brazil, Nogueira spent the latter part of her life in Britain. She always acknowledged her position as a foreigner, torn between two different cultures. In her work she is acutely aware of the fissures, the gaps that remain: 'I sometimes think that my work is all about gaps. For instance, you have routine in your life that carries on and then suddenly something happens, and that line is broken, and the "what happens then". What happens in that gap?'.

Like *Compass*, *Slip*, 1992 (p.61) both attracts and repels. An empty bell jar stands on a frosted glass plinth. It seems a perfect self-contained meeting of forms, until we notice that the bell jar's bottom edge is chipped, the jagged glass stained blood red. Suddenly there are several unanswered questions and possible narratives. The 'slip' of the title could suggest an accident but also perhaps a slip in meaning, a semantic gap between our visual experience and the words we have available to us. Nogueira's intensely human art searches for meaning at the points of breakdown, reflecting on the disjunctures between materials, language and experience.
AN

34
Slip
1992

35
(overleaf)
Compass
1993

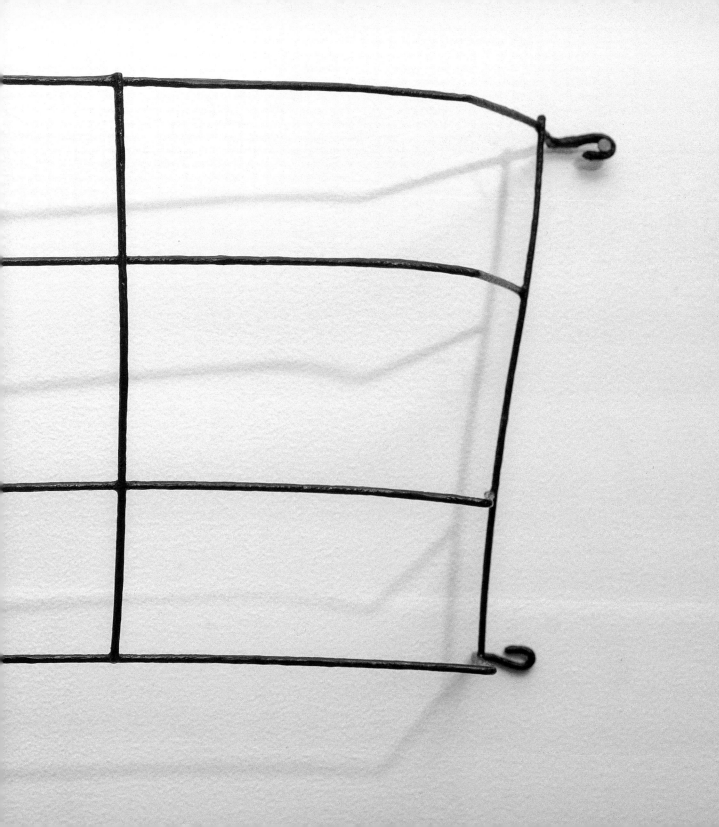

Anri Sala

Born 1974, Tirana, Albania
Lives and works in Paris, France

Reference
Anri Sala, de Appel Gallery, Amsterdam, 2000

Anri Sala works with film, manipulating the apparent verisimilitude of the filmed image to make work that is provocative, haunting and often extremely beautiful. He came to international prominence only recently, with a work called *Intervista*, 1998, in which he used a combination of found and newly-shot footage to probe the difference between the 'objective' reality of the film camera and the subjectivity of individual memory. Stumbling across a fragment from a television interview given by his mother in the 1970s, when she was one of the leaders of the Albanian Communist Youth Alliance, the artist confronted her with it. She remembered the interview, but could not enlighten her son as to the content of her speech – the sound track to the film was lost. He reconstructed it with the help of lip readers from a local school for the deaf, and showed the film to his mother again. She was at first horrified, disowning her own voice – 'I don't believe this. It's absurd…it's just spouting words!', but gradually began to accept her youthful self, and to try to explain her situation to her son – 'The commandments of Communism were to be honest, social-minded, idealistic, energetic, optimistic etc. …I was all of those things. I still am that way. And I still work for that today…I'm talking about a reality and my rapport with that reality which belongs to the past and concerns the present as well'.

Intervista documents the process through which Sala recovered the soundtrack of the film and the language spoken by his mother. Much of the ideology is clearly lost in translation – some of the words chosen by his mother to articulate her beliefs no longer have the same or even any meaning because the political system that guaranteed their intelligibility is no longer in existence. The film makes clear the potential for slippage between words as they are spoken, heard and understood. It also underlines the subjective and mutable nature of truth.

Truth plays a similarly important part in *Nocturnes*, 1999 (pp.67 – 69). In it, we meet two people from northern France. The first, Jacques, talks to the artist about the tropical fish with which he is obsessed. We see Jacques surrounded by fish in huge tanks, watching them, tending them, talking to them. The second man, Denis, we meet initially only in close-up. We see his hands, fidgeting incessantly as he talks about his experiences as a soldier for the UN in the Balkans. Where Jacques, charming if a little odd, confides in his audience, Denis, clearly disturbed, confesses to his: 'I started young, when I was eighteen, as soon as I was an adult I signed up. I was eighteen in July and I left in October. For a boy, life begins. So when you come back, you remember it and think about everything you've done over the last four years, when you did unusual things. You can't manage to say to yourself: on the 24th of July 1995 I killed four people. You think about it and you think about it and then you remember the four people you killed and the way you did it'. He can't say it to himself, but he says it to us, and it is obviously important that he is believed.

The two narratives begin separately, but the film cuts from one to another so that they begin first to overlap and then to merge. Though one is talking of his everyday reality and the other a nightmarish past from which he cannot seem to escape, both stories operate primarily in the present time of the film. Watching it, we cannot but notice similarities between the two men – Jacques tells us how the fish don't like to be looked at and how he himself has 'always felt like a Martian'. His sense of alienation from society chimes with that of Denis. Gradually, the two stories merge, so that it becomes difficult to tell which of the men is reliving past trauma and which is talking about his fish. The tone of the film becomes more and more anxious, as the viewer ceases to be a dispassionate observer and becomes absorbed in the simultaneous narrative of the two men.

As the two stories merge so do the images. As fish start to swim in and out of the animated cityscape in the violent PlayStation game played by the young ex-soldier, it becomes clear that what we are watching has shifted from neutral documentary into a meditation of the strategies individuals use to make sense of their position in the world. The nervous beauty of the filmed imagery captivates, at the same time as it induces a state of extreme anxiety.
FB

36
(pp.67–69)
transcript and stills from
Nocturnes
1999

I love all of them, but some I love more. I love the fosorochomistratus, the blue one in the middle, a bit dark, with his women with five spots along their bodies. Hup, she's just turned around. I like their mouths because they have a kind of permanent smile. But the mouth isn't for smiling, it's to go eating in the sand. They stick their heads in and filter everything, and then out through the gills, keeping the food. There are so many things to eat in sand.

When you've got a gun, you've got to take care of it. There, they tell you: you work with your gun, you sleep with it, you have sex with it. In the shower you turn it upside down and cover it with a towel. A gun is normal, so when you get here and you don't have it, it changes you. You have problems with people. I started young, when I was eighteen, as soon as I was an adult I signed up. I was eighteen in July and I left in October. For a boy, life begins. So when you come back, you remember it and think about everything you've done over the last four years, when you did unusual things. You can't manage to say to yourself: on the 24th of July 1995 I killed four people. You think about it and you think about it, and then you remember the four people you killed and the way you did it.

You see the father come out of the house but you can't see inside the house, only its shape. Then you see him go off, from above, you see him go to some other guys who are part of the militia, he picks up a gun, makes a sign and then it all comes down and you watch the bullet go.

That's what stops you sleeping. They don't warn you about that in training.

I've always felt like a Martian. Do you want some more? Ever since I was little I always felt like a Martian. Little Martians. Black ones, white ones, grey ones. The awful way people look at them.

I've noticed that a lot, and it scares me. I wanted to turn this into a shop, but I've stopped all that. I thought, it'll be great, people can come and see the fish's parents. Then one day five people turned up and all the fish swam away, hiding in the corners. I said to myself, that's awful.

Some of them can't handle it, that look. They stay in the corner and they usually get sick quite quickly.

If I remember right, I killed that person on the 13th of March 1995 at 5:28 in the evening. I remember everything. That one shocked me the most. It stops me sleeping every time I think of his face. It's a composite of that face – always from one side, then from the other and then facing with a hole in the head.

After four months, they've made you perfect. For four months you learn it all and then they send you off. You have a plan, to go and get some information, take some notes, look around a bit, and after three weeks you come back to base camp…

…and you write your report, you rest a bit, you put on the blue helmet instead of the beret. You drive the trucks, go and get the mail. That killed me, going to get the mail, what a laugh!

And the snipers' shots go ping-ting-ting-ting. It's great music! But I can't even wish it on the enemy. Really, I can't.

You see, it eats away at your life, it's in your face all at once. You can't live normally anymore. So you hold on to what you've got left. For me, it's the PlayStation.

You can see it when you put a new one in. If you put a new fish into a well-balanced tank, where each fish has found his space, without any precautions, the fish won't last an hour.

There are always small tensions, so to stop them becoming sources of stress or sickness, the fish spend their time avoiding each other, just looking at each other.

The sound here is everywhere and it's very stressful when sometimes it stops. It's awful. When the sound stops, I say to myself, oh shit, it's a disaster, they're all going to die. There's no more air, there's no more oxygen. Panic. In the middle of the night, at three in the morning, I wake up and come down. I can't hear the noise anymore; I can't hear the sound.

Basically, human beings aren't violent, they just like to dominate. You've got the brain's hemisphere you use, but violence is on the other side, true violence, barbarity, the capacity to destroy. They shave your head and show you films. Not the kind of film you get on TV. Different ways to kill. They put the information in and it becomes a reflex. And to stop you feeling remorse they inject you with something that makes you forget you're a human being.

It's always been like that, by stages, you have to. How do you find the right social balance, how do you do it. I observe things and think to myself, look, I'm not saying that humans are the same, but sometimes I think, well, there are similarities and to relate to human beings I still need to use other means.

Basically, I've got to stop. If I don't and keep it closed up inside me, it will grow inside me until it explodes, and that's when it gets dangerous.

Now I have my two lives, as it should be. In the evening I'm a kid, I put on my sports clothes and go and train in the park, then I come back. I have a shower and then I become a real kid in front of the PlayStation…

…and then I turn it off and go and live my day.

© Anri Sala, 1999

And the snipers' shots go
ping-ting-ting-ting.

Ann-Sofi
Sidén

Born 1962, Stockholm, Sweden
Lives and works in New York, USA
and Stockholm

References
*Ann-Sofi Sidén – Enquête: The Panning Eye
Revisited*, Paris Musées, Paris, 2001
Ann-Sofi Sidén: XXIV Bienal de São Paulo,
Moderna Museet, Stockholm, 1998

Worlds hidden from public view permeate the work of Ann-Sofi Sidén. Her film and video works of recent years have focussed on individuals whose lives are conducted out of sight, whose social interactions somehow sit outside the bounds of normality. She presents us with documentation, evidence of their activity, of their lives, often using the familiar black and white video technology of the surveillance camera to insist on the authenticity of what is shown to us. In installations such as *Who Told the Chambermaid*, 1998 and *Station 10 and Back Again*, 2001 such video footage is relayed on a bank of monitors, from a hotel and a fire station respectively. In each case the monitors are surrounded by related objects, some of which can be spotted in the locations depicted on video, further emphasizing the possible, though not certain, authenticity of the material before us. Rather than allow us to piece together a picture of the truth, however, Sidén makes us aware of the processes and mechanics of observation, of the desire to classify and delineate, of the boundary between observer and observed.

A poetic interweaving of factual and fictional components is the basis of Sidén's film, *QM, I Think I Call Her QM*, 1997 (pp.72–75), co-directed by Tony Gerber. The film originates in two distinct episodes in Sidén's previous work: the first is a series of performances Sidén realized in the late 1980s, where she appeared in a variety of social, public situations as the character, QM or Queen of Mud. QM is a mud-clad, primordial creature, whose origins, Sidén explains, lie in a research laboratory, where she was purportedly conceived to assist in an experiment. She is an object of study that has escaped her confines to scrutinize the world around her. The second starting point for the film was Sidén's indirect but remarkable encounter with the life of a New York psychiatrist, Alice E. Fabian. The late psychiatrist's Manhattan apartment was made available by her daughter to Sidén and a number of other artists for the exhibition *Who has enlarged this hole?* in 1994. Exploring the apartment, Sidén found several remnants of Fabian's life – diaries, tape recordings, etc. – all of which pointed to the gradual disintegration of her sanity towards the end of her life. The various records suggested that she had suffered from increasing mental and social alienation.

Sidén and Gerber's film, which brings the fictional QM character together with elements of the real life of Fabian, in a fictionalized character named Ruth Fielding, relates to both the relationship drama and the mystery as genres in film.

The film opens with a woman, Fielding, awaking from sleep, gradually collecting herself and her thoughts before she rises. Instantly recording her thoughts on tape, she utters the film's first words, 'I had the strangest dream', and throughout what follows there is a constant, inescapable sense of uncertainty as to whether what we are watching is real or imagined, part of the dream. This early reference to the subconscious operation of her mind coupled with the constant sense of temporal shifts – in the opening scene we slip from 3:05 am back to 2:00 am in the space of a few moments – enforce the sense of isolation that grows throughout the piece. Any encounter with the outside world is dealt with as hostile, even aggressive. All points of contact with the 'real' world seem at best tentative, if not entirely ruptured.

As she rises, Fielding discovers the mud creature under her bed, her unsurprised, even excited acceptance of the new arrival evident in her reaction, 'What have we here?'. The film proceeds to show us her unsuccessful attempts to control, care for and analyse the creature, who remains persistently silent. The tools of observation surround her and yet we know nothing of her. As Fielding observes her subject, so she is in turn observed from a distance by her curious neighbours. The film's claustrophobic, eerie atmosphere provokes a growing awareness that some schism has occasioned the imagined or actual arrival of the Queen of Mud in the doctor's world. Made manifest through some unknown breakdown, QM appears as a vessel for the expression of Fielding's skewed psyche, the result of an unknown trauma.
KB

A man from the phone company (Dennis Reid) calls at the door.

Dr Fielding (Kathleen Chalfant) recording her observations.

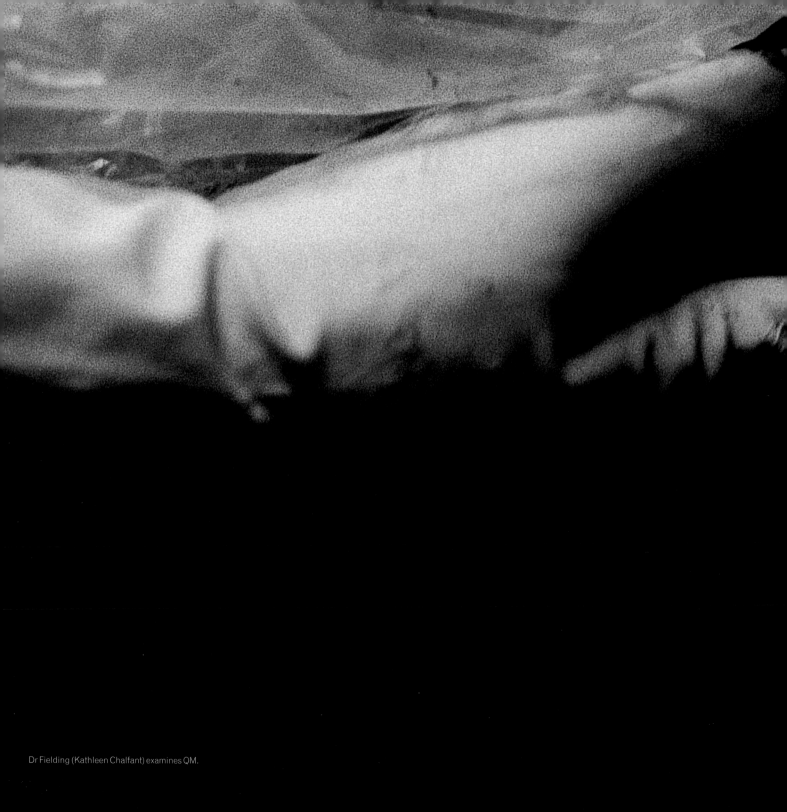

Dr Fielding (Kathleen Chalfant) examines QM.

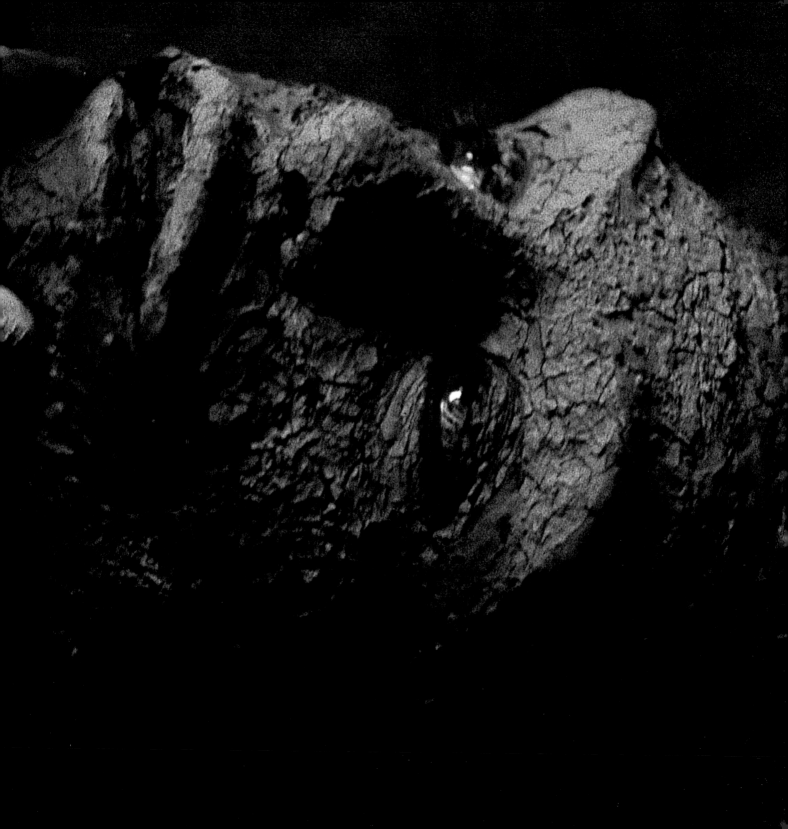

Christopher Wool

Born 1955, Chicago, USA
Lives and works in New York, USA

Reference
Christopher Wool, Carnegie Museum,
Pittsburgh, USA, 1999

Christopher Wool uses simple, readily-available techniques of mass reproduction – stencils and patterned paint rollers. His paintings recall Pop art's use of impoverished images and depersonalized means of production: Warhol's newspaper photographs or Lichtenstein's dots. His black on white works on aluminium are devoid of many of the traditional characteristics of painting – the weave of canvas or the spontaneous brushstroke. Stripped of colour, they are reduced to the most straightforward of mark-making. Works with both letter stencils and patterned rollers – designed to provide a cheap alternative to wallpaper – tend to connote deteriorated urban spaces, whether the decayed domestic interior or the sprawl of street graffiti. However sparse and reduced the means of their making, Wool's works persist in conveying a strong sense of aggression, even paranoia, an awareness of things not as they should be.

It is for his stark text works that Wool is perhaps best known, paintings in which words hover on the brink of disintegration into abstract forms.

The evenly-spaced letters, spread edge-to-edge across the surface of the painting, lack any punctuation. Stripped back to the basics in this way, the words become almost unreadable and the viewer is forced to work hard at establishing their meaning. The urge to read and to therefore understand, to decipher what appears written, is perpetually interrupted by the insistence on the letters as forms. When meaning does emerge, it is, as Thomas Crow has written, to 'recall the obsessive rants and catch-phrases of Travis Bickle-type casualties of the city. The very formality of the grids imposed upon the messages – indifferent to spacing, endings and sometimes superfluous letters – implies something of the schizophrenic's treatment of words as things'.

Several of Wool's works have featured the same quotation from the writings of a turn-of-the-century Russian intellectual, Vasili V. Rozanov. The text was referred to in a key Situationist text of 1967, Raoul Vaneigem's *The Revolution of Everyday Life*, as the definition of nihilism.

It describes a moment of irrevocable change, in which all semblance of normality is eradicated. In Wool's works, we are given access only to this moment. There is no way of knowing what follows or even what has preceded. The text is shockingly abrupt, immediately conveying a sense of panic and uncertainty, mirrored in the way in which the densely-packed letters do not easily resolve themselves into meaning.

Having explored various possibilities with the same text in three paintings made in 1990–91, Wool returned to it for *Untitled*, 1993 (p.79), a collaborative work made with Felix Gonzalez-Torres using the latter's signature form of the paper stack. The insistent repetition of the text through the piece amplifies and extends the resonance of the scenario it describes. The form given to the text at the same time encourages a more direct and active engagement on the part of the viewer, as the sheets can be taken away, like a souvenir, keeping the moment within constant reach.
KB

38
(overleaf)
Untitled (detail)
1991

39
Untitled
1993

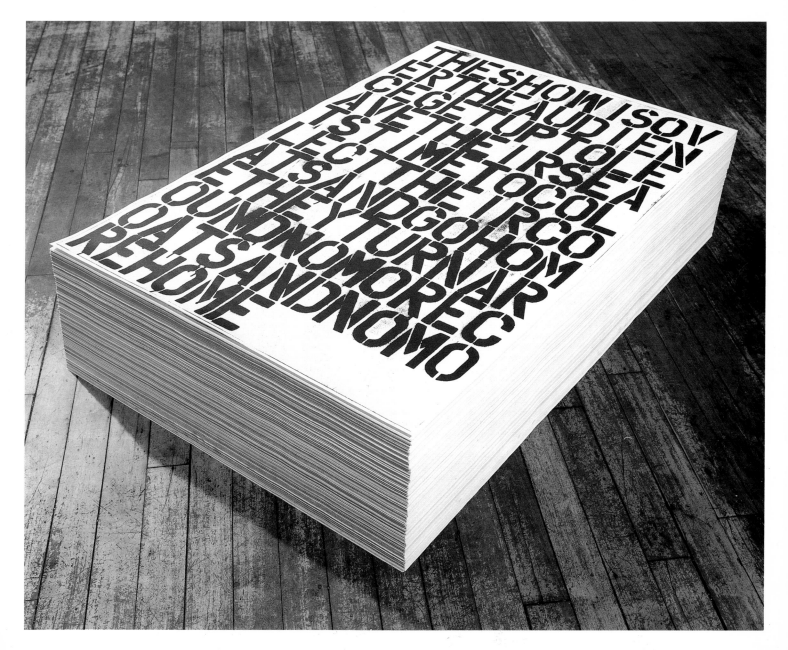

THE SHO

THE AUD

UP TO LEA

SEATS

VISOVER

ENCEGE

AVETHEI

METOCO

HRCON

List of Works

Page numbers refer to illustrations in this book

1 (p.12)
Martin Boyce
Something's Got to Give, 1995
screen print
96.5 x 70.5 cm
Courtesy the artist
© the artist and the Modern Institute,
Glasgow 2001

2 (p.13)
Martin Boyce
Now I've Got Worry (Storage Unit), 1997
nickel plated steel, birch plywood, plastic
laminates, fixtures and fittings, plywood
and paint
185 x 126 x 43 cm
Courtesy Modern Institute, Glasgow
© the artist and the Modern Institute,
Glasgow 2001

3 (pp.16–17)
Willie Doherty
Tell Me What You Want, 1996
two monitor video installation
dimensions variable
Running time: 10 minutes
Courtesy Matt's Gallery, London and
Alexander and Bonin, New York

4 (p.18)
Willie Doherty
Abandoned Interior II, 1997
cibachrome print mounted on aluminium
122 x 183 cm
Courtesy Matt's Gallery, London and
Alexander and Bonin, New York

5 (p.19)
Willie Doherty
Abandoned Interior III, 1997
cibachrome print mounted on aluminium
122 x 183 cm
Courtesy Matt's Gallery, London and
Alexander and Bonin, New York

6 (p.20)
Willie Doherty
Out of Sight, 1997
cibachrome print mounted on aluminium
122 x 183 cm
Courtesy Matt's Gallery, London and
Alexander and Bonin, New York

7 (p.21)
Willie Doherty
No Visible Signs, 1997
cibachrome print mounted on aluminium
122 x 183 cm
Courtesy Matt's Gallery, London and
Alexander and Bonin, New York

8 (pp.26–27)
Kendell Geers
Cry Wolf, 1999
sixty red emergency lights and cables
dimensions variable
Edition 1 of 3
Courtesy the artist and Stephen Friedman
Gallery, London; originally commissioned by
ArtPace / A Foundation for Contemporary Art,
San Antonio, Texas
Photograph: Elisabeth Scheder-Bieschin

9 (pp.24–25)
Kendell Geers
Double Time, 2000
installation with TV monitors and scaffolding
200 x 50 x 50 cm
Courtesy the artist and Stephen Friedman
Gallery, London

10 (p.30)
Felix Gonzalez-Torres
"Untitled", 1988
framed photostat
27.9 x 35.6 cm
Edition of 3
Courtesy Andrea Rosen Gallery, New York,
in representation of the Estate of Felix
Gonzalez-Torres
Photograph: Peter Muscato

11 (p.31)
Felix Gonzalez-Torres
"Untitled", 1988
framed photostat
26.7 x 29.8 cm
Edition of 1
Courtesy Andrea Rosen Gallery, New York,
in representation of The Estate of Felix
Gonzalez-Torres
Photograph: Peter Muscato

12 (p.33)
Felix Gonzalez-Torres
"Untitled" (We Don't Remember), 1991
offset print on paper (endless copies)
20.3 x 73.3 x 58.4 cm (at ideal height)
Hoffmann Collection, Berlin
Courtesy Andrea Rosen Gallery, New York,
in representation of The Estate of Felix
Gonzalez-Torres
Photograph: Mike Fear

13 (pp.2–3, 36–39)
Johan Grimonprez
dial H-I-S-T-O-R-Y, 1997
colour and black and white DVD projection
Running time: 68 minutes
Excerpts: *Mao II* and *White Noise* by Don DeLillo,
Wallacy Literary Agency Inc.
Original music and sample collage: David Shea
Production: Kunstencentrum STUC, Leuven
and Centre Georges Pompidou, MNAM, Paris
With the support of: *Documenta X*, Kassel;
Klapstuk 97, Leuven; Fundación Provincial de
Cultura, Diputación de Cádiz; The Fascinating
Faces of Flanders and the Ministry of the
Flemish Community, Brussels
Production DVD: incident vzw
Original Language: English
Translations: French, Dutch, German, Spanish,
Portuguese, Japanese, Galician

14 (pp.42–43)
Guillermo Kuitca
People on Fire, 1993
oil on canvas
123.2 x 194.3 cm
Collection of Craig and Ivelin Robins
Courtesy Sperone Westwater, New York

15 (p.45)
Guillermo Kuitca
Untitled, 1995
oil on canvas
196.2 x 195.6 cm
Private Collection
Courtesy Sperone Westwater, New York

16 (p.48)
Maria Lindberg
Abused Drawing, 1995-99
acrylic and dirt on paper
42 x 38 cm
Courtesy Andréhn-Schiptjenko, Sweden
Photograph: Mike Fear

17
Maria Lindberg
Girl in Reconstruction, 1996
acrylic on paper
45 x 38 cm
Courtesy Andréhn-Schiptjenko, Sweden

18
Maria Lindberg
Lost Friend, 1996
pencil on paper
45 x 38 cm
Courtesy Andréhn-Schiptjenko, Sweden

19
Maria Lindberg
A Hole to See the Wall Through, 1997
mixed media
38 x 45.5 cm
Courtesy Andréhn-Schiptjenko, Sweden

20
Maria Lindberg
A Last Glance of You, 1997
acrylic on paper
45 x 38 cm
Courtesy Andréhn-Schiptjenko, Sweden

21
Maria Lindberg
Long Ago and Far Away, 1997
pencil on paper
45 x 38 cm
Courtesy Andréhn-Schiptjenko, Sweden

22
Maria Lindberg
Wishes Come Through, 1997
acrylic on paper
36.5 x 34.5 cm
Courtesy Andréhn-Schiptjenko, Sweden

23
Maria Lindberg
Cure, 1998
pencil and acrylic on paper
45.5 x 38 cm
Courtesy Andréhn-Schiptjenko, Sweden

24 (p.49)
Maria Lindberg
Double Exposures (Milwaukee), 1998
acrylic on paper
37 x 38 cm
Courtesy Andréhn-Schiptjenko, Sweden
Photograph: Mike Fear

25
Maria Lindberg
Pieces of Reality, 1998
acrylic on paper
45 x 38 cm
Courtesy Andréhn-Schiptjenko, Sweden

26
Maria Lindberg
Red, White and Blue, 1998
acrylic on paper
51 x 73 cm
Courtesy Andréhn-Schiptjenko, Sweden

27
Maria Lindberg
Bloody Face, 1999
acrylic on paper
42 x 30.5 cm
Courtesy Andréhn-Schiptjenko, Sweden

28
Maria Lindberg
London Leaning Right, 1999
acrylic on paper
38 x 38 cm
Courtesy Andréhn-Schiptjenko, Sweden

29 (pp.50–51)
Maria Lindberg
Minutes Ago, 1999
acrylic on paper
31.5 x 44.5 cm
Courtesy Andréhn-Schiptjenko, Sweden
Photograph: Mike Fear

30
Maria Lindberg
The First Cut is the Deepest, 1999
acrylic on paper
38 x 45 cm
Courtesy Andréhn-Schiptjenko, Sweden

31
Maria Lindberg
As Above So Below, 2000
sound installation
Courtesy Andréhn-Schiptjenko, Sweden

32
Maria Lindberg
No Nothing, 2000
acrylic on paper
42 x 29 cm
Courtesy Andréhn-Schiptjenko, Sweden

33 (pp.54–57)
Tracey Moffat
Scarred for Life II, 1999
series of ten lithographs
offset print
80 x 60 cm
Edition of 60
Courtesy Victoria Miro, London

34 (p.61)
Lucia Nogueira
Slip, 1992
glass, red wax
94 x 41 x 41 cm
The Estate of Lucia Nogueira, courtesy
Anthony Reynolds Gallery, London

35 (pp.62–63)
Lucia Nogueira
Compass, 1993
metal, black wax
32 x 61 x 18.5 cm
The Estate of Lucia Nogueira, courtesy
Anthony Reynolds Gallery, London

36 (pp.67–69)
Anri Sala
Nocturnes, 1999
video projection
Running time: 11 minutes, 28 seconds
Courtesy Galerie Chantal Crousel, Paris

37 (pp.72–75)
Ann-Sofi Sidén
QM, I think I call her QM, 1997
DVD of 35 mm colour film with sound
Running time: 28 minutes
Co-directed by Tony Gerber
With Kathleen Chalfant, Ann-Sofi Sidén,
Emanuel Xuereb, Dennis Reid,
Paul Giangrossi and Ulf Lovén
Courtesy Galerie Nordenhake, Stockholm,
Berlin and the artist

38 (pp.80–81)
Christopher Wool
Untitled, 1991
Alkyd aluminium
220.5 x 147 cm
Courtesy the artist and Luhring
Augustine, New York

39 (p.79)
Christopher Wool in collaboration
with Felix Gonzalez-Torres
Untitled, 1993
offset print on paper (endless copies)
20.3 x 94 x 141 cm (at ideal height)
Hoffmann Collection, Berlin
Courtesy the artist and Luhring
Augustine, New York
Photograph: Peter Muscato